FRANCESCO GEMINIANI

THE ART OF PLAYING
ON THE VIOLIN

1751

Facsimile Edition

Edited, with an Introduction, by

DAVID D. BOYDEN

OXFORD UNIVERSITY PRESS

Music Department, 44 Conduit Street, London W. 1

CONTENTS

INTRODUCTION

THE following pages reproduce in facsimile a famous violin method, Geminiani's *The Art of Playing on the Violin* (Op. IX, London, 1751). First published just 200 years ago, Geminiani's treatise has for years been virtually impossible to obtain in an original edition, and while certain passages have been quoted again and again, the whole work has been read and studied relatively little in recent times.

Among other reasons, Geminiani's work has been neglected because it describes a technique quite different from that of the present. The publication of this facsimile and the recently published English translations of such treatises as those of Leopold Mozart and C. P. E. Bach may be attributed directly to an awakened interest in the details of eighteenth-century performance necessary to reproduce the sound of the music approximately as the composer intended. But one must never forget that the instructions given in eighteenth-century treatises are often meaningless or misleading when studied apart from the instruments of the time. In particular, the following facsimile will remain primarily a work of archaeological interest unless it is studied and practised by violinists who have taken the trouble to secure instruments and bows reconstructed according to conditions prevailing in the mid-eighteenth century (cf. footnote 2, p. vii).

The fame of this violin tutor rests not only on its historical position in violin playing but on the inherent value of its contents and on the occasional eloquence of its language. The claim that Geminiani's book is the first violin method has long since been abandoned, but it is none the less one of the first mature expositions of violin playing. Within the scope of its relatively few pages is covered quite completely the technical groundwork necessary to cope with almost any violinistic problem of its time except those posed by certain special effects and by music requiring an exceptional virtuosity such as the Locatelli Caprices.

Geminiani's treatise clearly shows the Italian origin of its contents (cf. *Notes concerning the Facsimile*, p. xii, note 4), and at the same time illuminates the considerable difference between the violin schools of France and Italy with respect to aesthetic ideas and technique, a difference that is part of the larger and recurrent struggle of French and Italian music in the eighteenth century. The early French violin school exhibited a pronounced interest in dance music and a strong descriptive tendency. In fact, the technical progress of French violin playing throughout the entire seventeenth century was impeded by the natural limitations of dance music and by the notion that music was good only in proportion as it portrayed something. The abstract idea of the Italian sonata was at first incomprehensible and foreign to the French. It was not until after 1750 that French aestheticians generally conceded that music need not necessarily represent anything in concrete terms. However, during the early years of the century some French composers tacitly admitted the validity of the Italian sonata by imitating it, for about 1720 a strong school of French 'sonatistes' appeared (e.g. Leclair). Thus by 1751, when Geminiani published his treatise, the rivalry between the French and Italian violin schools was somewhat less pronounced.

Even so, a residue of earlier antagonism may be observed in certain of Geminiani's remarks. A case in point is his opposition to the so-called 'Rule of Down Bow', codified by the French primarily for the correct bowing of dance music. This rule states in effect that the first note of every measure—or more generally, every metrically accented beat or part of a beat as far as the tempo permits—should be played down bow. Strictly applied, this rule often results in consecutive down or up bows. Geminiani's attitude towards such rational but restrictive discipline is one of furious impatience. In Example VIII he instructs the pupil to bow the music with alternate up and down bows 'taking Care not to follow that wretched Rule of drawing the Bow down at the first Note of every Bar'.

Geminiani also opposes the French tendency towards the idea of imitation in its most descriptive sense when he inveighs against 'imitating the Cock, Cuckoo, Owl, and other Birds; or the Drum, French Horn, Tromba-Marina, and the like'. Nevertheless, an imitation of a more musical and less naïve kind is implicit in several passages. He considers the perfect tone on the violin that which rivals the 'most perfect human voice'. Imitation of speech and oratory is implied when he says with respect to *piano* and *forte*: 'as all good Musick should be composed in Imitation of a Discourse, these two Ornaments are designed to produce the same Effects that an Orator does by raising and falling his Voice' (Example XVIII).

Of special significance is Geminiani's insistence on the role of emotional expression. His method contains important hints concerning the expressive style of playing the violin in the first part of the eighteenth century. Geminiani's expressive attitude permeates his remarks on certain ornaments and bow strokes as well as his whole general view of music. It is striking that Geminiani achieves an impressive eloquence, quite rare in violin treatises, largely in those passages concerning the emotional character of performance. For example, in the closing part of his description of the vibrato ('Close Shake') occur these remarkable words:

I would besides advise, as well the Composer as the Performer, who is ambitious to inspire his Audience, to be first inspired himself; which he cannot fail to be if he chuses a Work of Genius, if he makes himself thoroughly acquainted with all its Beauties; and if while his Imagination is warm and glowing he pours the same exalted Spirit into his own Performance. (Example XVIII, 14th section.)

In Geminiani's eyes the technique of playing the violin was inseparable from the expressive intention of any particular piece of music. Different manners of playing the same passage are linked to different types of emotional expression (i.e. the 'Affect'). His instructions with respect to the mordent ('Beat') begin 'This is proper to express several Passions'; and these passions, ranging from mirth to horror, depend for their expression on the manner of performing the mordent.

A similar range of emotions may be noted in his description of the manner of performing the vibrato, in itself one of the most expressive devices of violin playing. Geminiani's attitude towards the vibrato is prophetic of the future. For the first time in the violin treatises there occurs in his works a reference to some kind of continuous vibrato: 'when it [the vibrato] is made on short Notes, it only contributes to make their Sound more agreable [sic] and for this Reason it should be made use of as often as possible'. Several years earlier in his *Rules for Playing in True Taste* (Op. VIII), Geminiani not only makes the same remark, but emphasizes it by distinguishing between the incipient continuous vibrato, recommended for the violin, and the vibrato as a specific ornament which he finds more appropriate to the German flute. The vibrato of the latter, says Geminiani, 'must only be made on long Notes'. Thus with Geminiani the violin vibrato as a specific and occasional ornament is replaced by what is in principle the continuous vibrato.

A considerable latitude of expression is indicated also in the discussion of other technical matters. Of the numerous and varied bowings (cf. Example XX), none of the 'plain' bowings of individual notes, with the exception of semiquavers in Allegro, is considered good. It is the bowings with nuance and those with slurrings or mixtures of bowings that are superior. Geminiani's discussion of the appoggiatura, made indisputably clear by specific signs, shows that his normal concept of its performance was one of nuance from the appoggiatura to its main note. The length of this ornament is related to its 'Affect'. He clearly prefers an appoggiatura of unusual length which is 'supposed to express Love, Affection, Pleasure, etc.'. He allows for the short appoggiatura but 'it will lose much of the aforesaid Qualities'.

Geminiani's expressive ideas are not unique among violinists of the time; on the contrary, they were probably quite prevalent, especially among the Italians. In spite of the mysterious scarcity of Italian violin methods before 1750, other accounts of musicians, theorists, and aestheticians clearly suggest that the true manner of performing the music is submerged beneath the bare surface of the printed notes of the scores. The performing artist was expected to exert his imagination not only in an expressive performance 'according to the intentions of the composer' but also in improvising within the framework of the printed notes of the composition itself, especially in *Adagio* movements.

Corelli is a case in point. The notes of his printed scores suggest a dignified, simple, even austere music and a similar performance. But there is contemporary evidence that Corelli played his *Adagios* in a highly florid manner quite different from the printed notes, and that his manner of performance was a passionate one. The florid versions of the *Adagios* of Corelli's solo sonatas 'as he played them' were published in Amsterdam during his lifetime, and while their authenticity has been challenged, Pincherle in his book *Corelli* (1933) has demonstrated convincingly their probable genuineness. A vivid picture of Corelli as a performer is drawn by a contemporary:[1]

I never met with any man that suffered his passions to hurry him away so much whilst playing on the violin as the famous Arcangelo Corelli, whose eyes will sometimes turn as red as fire; his countenance will be distorted, his eyeballs roll as in agony, and he gives in so much to what he is doing that he doth not look like the same man.

It is in the sense of expressive performance as much as in the sense of technique that Geminiani preserves and furthers the Corelli tradition. In a broader sense, it is probable that *The Art of Playing on the Violin* of 1751 furnishes the key to the expressive and technical performance of Italian violin music of the first part of the eighteenth century. Nevertheless, Geminiani exhibits a cautious sobriety towards improvisation when he says 'playing in good Taste doth not consist of frequent Passages [i.e. florid improvisation], but in expressing with Strength and Delicacy the Intention of the Composer'; and later, 'were we to make Beats [mordents] and Shakes [trills] continually without sometimes suffering the pure Note to be heard, the Melody would be too much diversified'. But this is simply a warning against excess of established practice, for Geminiani and others left examples of their embellishment of certain fast as well as slow movements of Corelli's works.[2]

Compared to Leopold Mozart's *Versuch einer gründlichen Violinschule*, which appeared in 1756, Geminiani's treatise looks primarily to the past. Unlike Leopold Mozart, Geminiani makes no mention of certain matters which are related to the technical equipment of later violinists, for example, consecutive trills, and trills in thirds and even sixths. He says nothing of harmonics (also disliked by Leopold Mozart), or of preserving the same tone colour throughout a passage by using the higher positions on one string. While extensive, Geminiani's varieties of bowing, their execution, and the types of bowings indicated by dots and vertical strokes cannot be compared with their treatment in Leopold Mozart's book.

---

[1] François Raguenet, *Parallèle des Italiens et des Français*, 1702; English translation and footnotes attributed to J. E. Galliard, 1709. *The Musical Quarterly* for July 1946 reprinted the English translation (cf. p. 419).

[2] Geminiani's beautiful ornamented version of an *entire* sonata of Corelli (Op. V, no. 9) is printed in Sir John Hawkins's *A General History of the Science and Practice of Music* (reprinted, London, Novello, Ewer & Co., 1875), vol. ii, pp. 904–7.

Geminiani's manner of holding the violin is also relatively old-fashioned. Although the French edition of 1752 shows a violinist (Geminiani?) holding the violin under the chin, approximately in the centre over the tail-piece (string holder), this manner of holding the instrument is not that described either in the French or in the English text both of which recommend holding the violin at the collar-bone. Neither text says anything about holding the violin under the chin at the left side of the tail-piece, as is often claimed. By way of contrast, Leopold Mozart says that collar-bone position looks well but is insecure for the player; his preferred method is that of holding the violin under the chin at the right side of the tail-piece. The modern way of holding the violin under the chin at the left side of the tail-piece is advocated, apparently for the first time, by L'Abbé le Fils (J. Saint-Sévin) in his *Principes du violon* (1761). To be sure, the German translation of Geminiani's treatise tells the violinist to hold the instrument 'between the collarbone and the jawbone' with the chin 'at the right and not at the left side of the string-holder'. But this translation could not have been issued before 1785 (see footnote 2, p. x), more than twenty years after Geminiani's death in 1762.[1] However, in view of the technical demands of the vibrato and of shifting, which in his examples require occasional awkward and large movements of the hand, Geminiani must have had an extraordinary facility in holding the instrument with his thumb and index finger; perhaps he lapsed occasionally into the position shown in the frontispiece of the French edition of 1752, reproduced on the cover of this book.

Geminiani advocates the typical Italian bow grip of the first part of the eighteenth century. The French grip, which gradually became obsolete after 1725, placed the thumb under the hair of the bow with three fingers on the stick and the little finger sometimes bracing on the player's side of the stick. In contradistinction, Geminiani grasped the bow with the four fingers and the thumb, which was inserted between the bow stick and the hair. According to his text, the bow is 'to be held at a small distance from the nut [frog]', but the frontispiece of the French edition shows the hand at a considerable distance from the nut of the bow. Strength of tone comes from pressure by the index finger which, in the frontispiece at least, grasps the bow at the first joint. Although Geminiani's bow grip is 'modern' compared to the French grip, it is not that of the advanced school. For the latter one must look to Leopold Mozart, who describes a firmer grip in which the bow stick is grasped 'at its lowest extremity between the thumb and the middle joint of the index finger, or even a little behind

it'. As Mozart says, this grip permits a more robust tone, an ideal which is that of a later time.

Another traditional feature of Geminiani's method is his inclusion of the fingerboard 'for learners' (Example IA). His information on the intonation system is also more proper to the past in that in enharmonic pairs of notes he indicates such notes as G sharp lower in pitch than A flat (cf. Examples II and IV). By way of paradox, these enharmonic distinctions may possibly account for Geminiani's 'advanced' chromatic fingerings, discussed below.

Viewed against the whole panorama of violin technique in the eighteenth century,[2] Geminiani's horizon is relatively limited, but on occasions his imaginative and inventive mind intuitively foresaw the future. He appreciated the inherent expressive possibilities of the continuous vibrato. By a single simple illustration, later known as the 'Geminiani' grip (see Example IB), Geminiani clarified and standardized for each individual player the correct position of the fingers of the left hand on the fingerboard of the violin. Significantly, Leopold Mozart adopts Geminiani's grip in the second edition of his *Violinschule* (1769–70), although it is absent from the first (1756). Geminiani's instructions with respect to fingering each note of chromatic passages with a separate finger was so far in advance of his time that this fingering had to be rediscovered in the twentieth century by Joseph Achron and expounded by Carl Flesch.

Some of Geminiani's information is less revolutionary in implication, but it reflects relatively advanced practices. In his text and musical examples, Geminiani indicates seven playing positions of the hand ('orders'). Of particular interest is the example illustrating double stops that necessitates the use of the seven 'orders' on *all four* strings. In his twelve compositions, however, Geminiani is somewhat more conservative.

Geminiani's invention and experimental attitude are shown in his fingerings for shifts. The various fingerings which are used to shift from one position to another appear to aim at presenting every possible solution. The result of such systematic completeness is a bewildering confusion of choice. If any single dominating principle can be observed among the numerous fingerings for shifts, it is that the number of shifts is reduced by favouring shifts involving larger movements of the hand (e.g. fingerings 1 2 3, 1 2 3; or 1 2 3 4, 1 2 3 4). Geminiani includes but does not emphasize fingerings that are more 'modern' in that they involve smaller movements of the hand in the interest of greater legato and better intonation.

The same kind of systematic completeness may be

---

[1] The date of Geminiani's death is firmly established, but the date of his birth has been the subject of much speculation. In 1934 the late Adolfo Betti finally showed beyond reasonable doubt that Geminiani was born in 1687. See Adolfo Betti, *Francesco Geminiani* (Stabilimento grafico, A. M. Amedei, Lucca, 1934), p. 9. Betti's larger work on Geminiani (*La Vita e l'arte di Francesco Geminiani*) was announced for publication in 1933 but it never appeared. The whole chronology of Geminiani's life should be re-examined.

[2] For background details, including those of the eighteenth-century violin and bow, see David D. Boyden, 'The Violin and its Technique in the 18th Century' (in *The Musical Quarterly* for Jan. 1950). For a modern reconstruction of violin and bow according to eighteenth-century playing conditions, see Sol Babitz, 'Telltale Marks on Old Violins' (*The Etude* for Aug. 1951). For intonation systems, see David D. Boyden, 'Prelleur, Geminiani, and Just Intonation' (*The Journal of the American Musicological Society*, Fall, 1951).

observed in his scales, in broken scales including skips over a string, and particularly in the variety of his fingerings for double stops. He gives all the possible double stops up to and including the octave (Example XXII) and including those unisons that require a whole tone extension of the little finger. Parenthetically, it is significant with respect to the performance of triple and quadruple stops, that chords involving three and four notes are shown mainly as arpeggiated (Example XXI).

His bowing variants of set passages exhibit a surprising variety of strokes (Examples IX, XVI, and XVII). Geminiani's first bowing exercise on the open strings (Example XXIV) can be and is used profitably at the present day. But Geminiani's attitude towards the desirability of certain bow strokes and their execution is difficult to understand. His Example XX classifies the various bow strokes with such designations as 'good', 'bad', and 'middling'. On what grounds these distinctions are made is not clear beyond the fact that bow strokes of individual notes without nuance are generally considered mediocre. Even more puzzling is his attitude towards the staccato in which 'the bow is taken off the strings at every note'. The use of this stroke is considered 'good' only for a series of staccato quaver notes in Allegro and Presto; all other examples of the staccato are labelled 'bad' or 'particular'. Strangest of all, Geminiani makes no provision whatever for detached strokes played on the string, the normal violin staccato of the eighteenth century. Can it be that the latter is lurking under Geminiani's sign (⁄) which indicates that 'the notes are to be play'd Plain and the Bow is not to be taken off the Strings'? If so, Geminiani admits no 'plain' legato stroke. Finally, Geminiani considers dots over notes under slurs 'particular', but in his text he does not even mention this bowing or its execution.

A remark of some interest concludes his text on bowing. He warns against marking time with the bow, and says 'in playing Divisions, if by your Manner of Bowing you lay a particular Stress on the Note at the beginning of every Bar, so as to render it predominant over the rest, you alter and spoil the true Air of the Piece, and except where the Composer intended it, and where it is always marked, there are very few Instances in which it is not very disagreeable'. Geminiani is exceptional in his protest against metrical accent, the use of which was commonly recommended in treatises of the time.

In presenting the material, Geminiani's text sets forth almost too briefly the basic information, illustrated by long music examples and complete pieces whose execution Geminiani leaves largely to the student. In using Geminiani's work most violin pupils would need a good teacher without whom the problem of applying the basic principles of the text to the lengthy examples and the music would be too great for the average student's persistence and imagination. Geminiani's work has the important virtue of a carefully ordered subject-matter that taken as a whole is systematic and relatively complete for his time. But it is unfortunate that his treatise suffers from a text that is inadequate in its explanation of the technical possibilities suggested by the music and particularly by the examples.

As a result, Geminiani's treatise cannot be appreciated by a reading of the text alone. The latter by itself conceals the true technical magnitude of the work as a whole. The text comments not at all upon the great variety of fingerings for shifts indicated in the examples. Extensions of the fingers are required in the examples of double stops, but the text says nothing about them. The same is true concerning mysterious contractions of the hand (e.g. fingerings 1 3 4 or 1 2 4 on successive chromatic half-steps), apparently to facilitate shifting to lower positions, perhaps necessary when the violin is held at the collar-bone without the firmness of chin support. The same paucity or total lack of textual explanation may be noted with respect to certain technical problems inherent in numerous passages in the examples: fingering changes within single notes of double stops, the use of the modern half-position fingering, use of the open string, and the surprising range of modulation in Example XV.

While much must be inferred from the examples and the music, the text is sometimes quite explicit. His detailed explanation of the use of the wrist, arm, and shoulder, and their use in the bow strokes at different tempi is a model of clarity and conciseness. Geminiani is also sometimes explicit about pedagogy. He appreciated the beginner's problem of co-ordinating the complicated physical movements of the right and left hand, and with this in mind, he recommends that the difficulties of the left hand be practised first and separately, deferring the bowing problem until Example VII.

In certain ways Geminiani's text has the virtue of its defects. Geminiani must have realized that the very lack of concrete and mechanistic detail would force students to a healthy exercise of imagination and self-reliance in performing the examples and the music. Interpreted in this light, his text contains frequent instances of laconic and masterly understatement. Concerning his double-stop example (XXII) Geminiani says, 'Those who, with Quickness and Exactness, shall execute this Example, will find themselves far advanced in the Art of playing double Stops'. The same attitude may be observed in Geminiani's brief remark about the twelve pieces which follow the examples. He says, 'I have not given any Directions for performing them; because I think the Learner will not need any, the foregoing Rules and Examples being sufficient to qualify him to perform any Musick whatsoever'.

The music given in Geminiani's treatise suggests that many current notions about him are based more on the random and casual evidence of the eighteenth century than on an examination of his music.[1] A want of invention is

---

[1] The most thorough discussion of Geminiani's music may be found in Marion E. McArtor's *Francesco Geminiani Composer and Theorist* (unpublished doctoral dissertation, University of Michigan, Ann Arbor, Michigan, 1951).

not evident either in his musical materials nor in the variety of types of pieces given in the following facsimile. As Geminiani says in his preface, there are 'twelve Pieces in different Stiles'. Among them are pieces in slow 'pathetic' style full of expressive nuance. Several of the pieces are dances; and although they are not labelled as such, one may recognize readily enough a *Corrente*, a *Gigue*, and a *Gavotte* (Composition VIII). The latter is really a *Gavotte en rondeau*, of which the *Gavotte* proper is distinguished by a chromatic descending bass. Of the several quasi-fugal pieces, the best is Composition XII, modelled on the fugues in Corelli's solo violin sonatas (Op. V). Compared to Corelli's fugues, Geminiani's fugue is more advanced violinistically and more dramatic musically. Besides these types there are individual pieces of concerto character specializing in scales and in figures peculiar to the violin. Unlike Corelli's sonatas, the pieces of Geminiani are all in one movement. Still, it is possible that Geminiani's three successive pieces each in B minor (IX, X, XI) are intended to comprise a single *sonata da chiesa*.

The slow pieces are primarily expressive in character, but the fast pieces exhibit considerable boldness and dramatic power. To the usual violin resources of arpeggiated figures played across or skipping strings, Geminiani adds figures abruptly contrasting the high and low registers of the violin, as well as special bowings which involve syncopations, chromatic sequences, and even those bowings that use vertical strokes and dots under slurs.

The prominent role of the continuo itself is a considerable factor in the dramatic effect of some of these pieces. The continuo is frequently of true obligato character and sometimes rivals in interest the solo part itself. In Composition V in particular the high register of the violoncello (expressly designated) is exploited, and its occasional penetration into the violin register, where it sometimes momentarily sounds above the violin, shows Geminiani's interest in instrumental colour and sonority. In the fugal pieces, the continuo shares in the imitation, although as a rule it reinforces the lower note of the double stops in the solo violin. The interest attached to the continuo is implied by the fact that dynamic markings are given for the continuo, a quite unusual practice.

Besides the dynamic indications in the continuo, certain special effects are suggested by Geminiani's distinctive use of *piano* and *forte*. In addition to the usual echo effect of repeating a passage softly, Geminiani expressly indicates at times that passages are to be played continuously loud or continuously soft. For instance, Composition IV has a *forte* expressly marked over the first note of seven successive measures, apparently to emphasize the chromatic progression of the harmony. Consecutive use of *piano* occurs also. An even more curious dynamic marking is indicated in Composition IX where three short phrases in stepwise ascending sequence are marked *p, non tanto, for.*, apparently meaning *piano, mezzo forte, forte*—or perhaps even a continuous crescendo.

There are occasional rich harmonic effects. Besides the chromatic passages in the melodic line, certain altered chords, for instance the Neapolitan-sixth chord and more rarely the augmented-sixth chord, are used with telling effect.

With the exception of two or three sectional dance pieces, the compositions given here have a continuous flow intimately connected with their highly integrated forms. Some of these are contrapuntal or quasi-fugal. Others are composed of melodic materials that are not sharply contrasted in character and that form a *continuum* which appears to be constructed out of music naturally evolving from itself. But, as in the case of J. S. Bach, one does not sense a monotony from this closely related material. Besides, the contrast of the underlying changes of key, which do not necessarily coincide with changes of melodic material, contributes a subtle variety. It is noticeable that the new key is introduced strikingly soon after the first statement. The opening and closing tonic sections are quite brief; the middle sections of these pieces are devoted as a rule to modulation through several closely related keys.

These compositions, rooted in the continuity of counterpoint and in figured-bass harmony, can be regarded as mature expressions of Baroque music. They have much less relation to the Classic sonata of the later eighteenth century. In this sense of working within the mould of the past, Geminiani is a conservative in his music as well as in his exposition of violin technique.

But historical criticism of this sort must not be construed as a qualitative judgement. If the perfection of anything depends on the degree to which worth-while ideas find their most appropriate formal expression, Geminiani's music and technical information contained in his violin treatise deserve high praise. Geminiani, if not a genius, was more than a man of talent. His true stature has been obscured for years by the faint praise of Burney and Hawkins and by unreliable eighteenth-century anecdotes. But in the facsimile that follows Geminiani may speak for himself through the text, examples, and music of *The Art of Playing on the Violin*.

THE VIOLIN TREATISES OF GEMINIANI

THE violin treatises attributed to Geminiani are remarkably numerous. To this fact and to their protean powers of change and reproduction may be ascribed the present incredible confusion concerning their dates and contents. The impressive number of 'Geminiani' violin methods comprises (1) those works indisputably genuine, their translations and edited versions; (2) those anonymous works attributed to him and appearing during his lifetime; and (3) those posthumous works that rightly or wrongly bear his name, and that are based largely on the anonymous methods just mentioned.

The first group includes Geminiani's most important work on violin playing, *The Art of Playing on the Violin* (Op. IX, London, 1751), the facsimile of which follows. In 1752 this work appeared in Paris as *L'Art de jouer le violon*.[1] Except for a few minor changes, the translation is a faithful one, and the examples and music are almost identical. However, Geminiani's entertaining and informative preface in the original edition is omitted, and by way of compensation, a valuable frontispiece, showing Geminiani (?) playing the violin, is added to the French edition. In 1769, an abbreviated version of the 1751 work was published in the United States under the title *An Abstract of Geminiani's Art of Playing on the Violin* (Boston, New-England, Printed by John Boyles). Later, a German translation, *Gründliche Anleitung oder Violinschule* was published by Artaria in Vienna.[2] The claim that there was a Dutch translation is apparently without substance. About or shortly after 1800 at least one edition appeared that was subject to editing and 'improvement' conforming to the demands of a more advanced violin technique: *L'Art du violon ou méthode raisonnée* (Sieber, Paris; no date, but Eitner gives 1803). The title-page says explicitly 'Composée primitivement par le Célèbre F. Geminiani', and the contents show extensive changes from the original.

The second group of treatises, those published anonymously during Geminiani's lifetime, bear a family resemblance to Peter Prelleur's *The Modern Musick-Master* (1731), Part V of which is entitled *The Art of Playing on the Violin*.[3] The fact that the latter title is identical with that of Geminiani's 1751 work has created the legend that these two works are 'virtually identical', an opinion which completely disregards their different character. Actually there is no conclusive proof that Prelleur Part V and the works modelled on it were written by Geminiani.

Prelleur Part V gives the most elementary instruction, a considerable part of which is not primarily concerned with violin playing. The only complex part of this work

is the fingering chart which indicates hand position and which shows twenty notes to the octave, indicating differences in enharmonic pairs, such as D sharp and E flat. In general, the 1751 work is for advanced players of the time; Prelleur Part V is for beginners and for amateurs.

The Modern Musick-Master enjoyed a considerable popularity (4th edition, 1738), and the individual parts were frequently reprinted, at least as late as the 1750's. Thus there are several examples of separate printings of Part V that, except for the title-pages, have been issued from the same plates as Prelleur. Since *The Modern Musick-Master* was compiled by Prelleur from different anonymous authors, at least one of whose treatises was pirated by Prelleur from a work already in print,[4] one might argue that these anonymous works, identical with Part V, actually antedated Prelleur. But such an argument is untenable because the dates of the publishers concerned are all later than 1731. If there was an earlier model for Prelleur Part V, it has not yet come to light. Heron-Allen assigns the date *circa* 1720 to one of these anonymous works, but in view of more recent research, the work in question was probably published between 1734 and 1738.[5]

In addition, there are anonymous works whose contents are nearly identical with Prelleur Part V, but which have been issued from different plates, with a different title-page and frontispiece, and with different pieces of music. Such a work is *The Compleat Tutor for the Violin* (London, J. Simpson, 174–?). Unlike the posthumous compilations described below, the work just mentioned reproduces the fingering chart of Prelleur quite accurately.

In the third group of 'Geminiani' tutors are those posthumous works that are explicitly ascribed to him. The publication of these works may be explained by the popularity of Prelleur Part V. They differ externally from Prelleur in various respects: in typography, in the frontispieces which (according to Heron-Allen) exhibit costumes of a later period, in the format which is lengthwise, in

---

[1] The date does not occur on the title-page, but both Eitner (*Quellen-Lexikon*) and La Laurencie (*L'École française de violon*, vol. iii, p. 22) give 1752.

[2] The German translation must have been published between 1785 and 1805. See Karl Gerhartz, *Die Violinschule in ihrer musikgeschichtlichen Entwicklung bis Leopold Mozart*, published in *Zeitschrift für Musikwissenschaft*, Jahrgang vii (Oct. 1924–Sept. 1925), pp. 553–69. This translation is for the most part an accurate, but much less eloquent, version of the 1751 work. Such additions and omissions as occur ostensibly adapt the original to the changing times.

[3] The date 1731 (or 1730 in some copies) is clearly printed on the title-page of *The Modern Musick-Master*, although Prelleur's name does not appear. However, *The Oxford History of Music* (vol. iv, p. 175, note) claims that information in Frank Kidson's *British Music Publishers* (1900) indicates that Prelleur cannot have been published before 1734. On the contrary, nothing in Kidson makes the date 1731 improbable. Sir John Hawkins (see note 2, p. vi above: vol. ii, p. 896) says that Prelleur was hired by Cluer and Dicey 'about the year 1730' to compile the work. Kidson (p. 29) thinks that Cluer published 'as late as 1729–30' and that Dicey was his immediate successor. In addition, *The Modern Musick-Master* was announced in *Foy's Weekly Journal* for 14 Nov. 1730. See Dayton C. Miller, *Catalogue of Books and Literary Materials relating to the Flute* (Cleveland, 1935), p. 78.

[4] According to Dayton C. Miller (see note 3, above), Prelleur's sec-

tion on the German flute is a pirated edition of the English translation (1729) of Hotteterre le Romain's *Principes de la flûte traversière* (1707).

[5] Edward Heron-Allen, *De Fidiculis Bibliographia*, London, 1890–4, vol. ii, p. 302, (no. 713). Heron-Allen's dating was unduly influenced by the costumes of the frontispiece. The title-page of this work lists the publishers as T. Cobb and John Simpson. According to Kidson (see note 3, above), T. Cobb followed Cluer and Dicey (see note 3, above), and published about the years 1734–8, dates that are consistent with those of John Simpson.

It should in no way detract from Heron-Allen's monumental achievement to point out that some of his dates should now be revised in light of more recent information, particularly that of Kidson. With respect to the following listings, pertinent to the discussion, these corrections should be made: no. 713—see above; no. 715—Anonymous, *Compleat Tutor* (London, Peter Thompson) must be *c.* 1751 NOT 1780; no. 793—Geminiani, *Compleat Instructions* (London, J. Longman & Co.) must be 1767–70 NOT 1740; no. 794—Geminiani, *The Art of Playing on the Violin*; Heron-Allen mentions a second edition, 1791, by Bremner (the source of this information cannot be traced. It is probably an error. Bremner died in 1789); no. 796—Geminiani, *L'Art de Jouer* (Paris) should be 1752 NOT *c.* 1730; no. 797—Geminiani, *L'Art du Violon ou Méthode raisonnée* (Paris, Sieber) should be *c.* 1803 NOT *c.* 1750.

the inaccurate reproduction of the fingering chart, in differences in the concluding pieces of music, and in the fact that the title-page claims Geminiani as author. Their information is drawn mainly from Prelleur to which is frequently added the table of ornaments from Geminiani's 1751 work.

These compilations are clearly the doings of publishers anxious to profit from an established name and from a work that had sold well for years. The fact that these methods were issued after Geminiani's death (1762) may be demonstrated conclusively by the dates of the publishers issuing the works (cf. Kidson; see footnote 3, p. x) and by the internal evidence of various pieces that are included: for instance, excerpts from Monsigny's *Deserter* (1769) and Gretry's *Richard the Lion Hearted* (1784).

In view of their elementary information, dating largely from 1731, the popularity of these methods can be explained only by the phenomenon of the rise of the amateur and by the wide gulf between him and the professional performer, a state of affairs that became general after 1750. If this were not the case, it would be impossible to explain the considerable sale of the following works in an era that witnessed the Tourte bow, the technique of Viotti, and the advanced methods of the later eighteenth century. Among these 'Geminiani' compilations are:[1]

1. *New and Compleat Instructions for the Violin* (London, Longman & Broderip, 178–?).
2. *Compleat Tutor for the Violin* (London, S. A. & P. Thompson, 178–?).
3. *Entire New and Compleat Tutor for the Violin* (London, J. Preston, 178–?).
4. *Compleat Instructions for the Violin* (London, G. Goulding, 1790?).

In spite of differences of detail, these works are all substantially the same.[2] The differences of content are those of the frontispiece, a small deletion or addition here and there, and a different set of complete pieces at the end. A typical description of the latter is 'the finest Rigadoons, Almands, Sarabands, Courants and Opera Airs extant'. The four titles above are probably a mere sampling of the posthumous Geminiania that may still be extant; works of this order continued to appear as late as the early nineteenth century: *New and Compleat Instructions for the Violin* (London, M. Clementi, c. 1806).

To summarize the chronology of the violin tutors described above: after the anonymous Part V of Prelleur's *The Modern Musick-Master* appeared in 1731 (or 1730), it was reissued, still as an anonymous work, either from the original plates or from new plates made by different publishers but copied almost word for word from Prelleur Part V. This situation continued at least to the 1750's.

Whether there was an earlier model for Prelleur Part V or whether the latter was actually written by Geminiani is not known. At any rate, Geminiani's name appears on none of the extant works derived from Prelleur Part V until after Geminiani's death in 1762. Heron-Allen's dating (see note 5, p. x) which appears to contradict this statement is an error. The only violin tutors that are indisputably by Geminiani and over which he had complete control are the 1751 work, here printed in facsimile, and its French translation of 1752.

After 1762 a large number of 'Geminiani' violin tutors appeared and continued to appear for over forty years thereafter. These were nothing but versions of Prelleur Part V supplemented by Geminiani's own table of ornaments taken from the 1751 works (the table also appeared in other of Geminiani's works). This *mélange* was sold under the name of Geminiani. The advantage of using his name for sales' purposes is obvious, but it is not clear whether the publishers felt some justification for doing so either because they included the Geminiani table of ornaments or because they believed that Geminiani really was the author of Prelleur Part V.

Whatever the reason, Geminiani's death removed any possibility of protest concerning the continuing issuance under his name of works that, in view of the advanced material contained in the 1751 work, could not have represented his attitude towards violin playing much later than 1731, if at all. In fairness to Geminiani's reputation, any estimate of his position in violin pedagogy should be based not on the anonymous or posthumous 'Geminiania' but exclusively on the 1751 work, the facsimile of which follows and which is now reprinted, as far as is known, for the first time in 200 years.

NOTES CONCERNING THE FACSIMILE

1. The facsimile is reproduced exactly from the clearer of the two copies in the British Museum,[3] with the reservation that a small reduction in page size, of about one-tenth in the music and slightly more in the text, has been made. The idea of reproducing this facsimile in a format similar to that of the French edition (where the appropriate example follows directly after the text that it illustrates) was abandoned because of technical difficulties. However, the valuable frontispiece of the French edition is included on the cover of this facsimile edition.

2. Such typographical errors as occur in the original are for the most part obvious and easy to correct. No attempt has been made to list them.

---

[1] These dates, which should be considered approximations, are those given in catalogues issued by the Library of Congress: Julia Gregory, *Catalogue of Early Books on Music* (Washington, 1913), and Hazel Bartlett, *Supplement* (Washington, 1944). The dates in these catalogues are confirmed by the information in Kidson.

[2] The Library of Congress copy of *Compleat Instructions for the*

Violin has a particular historical interest in that it must have been used in the United States until 1800 at least, judging by the chronology of certain tunes copied by hand into the back of the book. Among these tunes are *Boston March* (1799-1800), *President's New March* (1796), and *Yankee Doodle* (c. 1795?).

[3] By courtesy of the Trustees.

3. The notation may be puzzling on occasions: the notation of accidentals generally follows the old rule that an accidental is not valid for an entire measure but only for the first note affected and for the same note if immediately repeated. The latter rule also applies to notes repeated over the bar line.

The notation of some double stops and most triple and quadruple stops is approximate with respect to the duration of time values indicated.

The text and the examples (XVIII, XIX) that explain the appoggiatura use the notation ♪ only. However, in some of the other examples ♪ is used as well; and in the compositions, ♪ is used most frequently, ♪ often, and ♩ occasionally to indicate the appoggiatura. An analysis of the musical context of these different types of notation shows that the ♪ appoggiatura is used for the most part before notes of relatively short duration; ♪ mainly before quaver, crotchet, or dotted-crotchet notes; and four of the five instances of the ♩ appoggiatura occur before minims. Although an indifference to distinctions of notation is suggested by a few cases where identical passages are written with different types of appoggiatura notation, Geminiani's notation as a whole shows a tendency toward the advanced practice (cf. C. P. E. Bach) of indicating through the notation itself the relative length of the appoggiatura. In a few cases one may ask whether Geminiani intended a 'passing' appoggiatura, that is, an appoggiatura before the beat (e.g. the opening of Example XIII).

4. The Italian captions, markings, and abbreviations found in the examples and music seem to indicate that the plates engraved for them were prepared in Italy. If so, why, and especially when, was this done? Many details of Geminiani's life are still obscure, but as far as is known, he came to England about 1714 and did not return to Italy.

Could the examples and music, and perhaps the text, have been prepared for an Italian edition prior to 1714? In view of the advanced technique implied in the examples, such a possibility is unlikely. Besides, such mature pedagogy could hardly be expected from a man not more than 27. If the text is a translation from an Italian original it was done by a man with a thorough and sometimes extraordinary command of English. Hence if Geminiani himself translated from the Italian or wrote the text originally in English he must have done so after long residence in England. Of course, the work may have been translated by someone else. The fact that all the text appears in one place followed by all the examples and music (whereas in the French edition of the following year each part of the text is followed immediately by its appropriate example) suggests the possibility that the plates for the examples and music were prepared in Italy first and that the text was written afterwards. However, until further details of Geminiani's life are known, any answer to the above questions is pure conjecture.

The meaning of almost all the Italian terms used in the examples and music is made clear in the text. Two possible exceptions are (1) *Traspne* (Trasposizione): that is, a shift of hand position (Example XV); and (2) 'g' for down bow and 's' for up bow are the Italian abbreviations for 'giù' and 'su', respectively.

5. The facsimile shows the original pagination: the pages of the text are numbered 1–9; then the music examples and compositions are numbered 1–51. This manner of numbering supports the point suggested above: namely, that the text was prepared at a different place (and perhaps time) from the examples and the compositions.

Berkeley, California.   David D. Boyden

I gratefully acknowledge the assistance of Professor Arthur Mendel (Princeton University) and of Mr. Sol Babitz (Los Angeles), both of whom read the MS. of the Introduction and offered valuable advice.

D.D.B.

The Art of

Playing on the

VIOLIN

Containing

All the Rules necessary to attain to
a Perfection on that Instrument, with
great variety of Compositions, which
will also be very useful to those who
study the Violoncello, Harpsichord &c.

Composed by

F. Geminiani

Opera. IX.

LONDON: MDCCLI.

PREFACE.

THE Intention of Mufick is not only to pleafe the Ear, but to exprefs Sentiments, ftrike the Imagination, affect the Mind, and command the Paffions. The Art of playing the Violin confifts in giving that Inftrument a Tone that fhall in a Manner rival the moft perfect human Voice ; and in executing every Piece with Exactnefs, Propriety, and Delicacy of Expreffion according to the true Intention of Mufick. But as the imitating the Cock, Cuckoo, Owl, and other Birds ; or the Drum, French Horn, Tromba-Marina, and the like ; and alfo fudden Shifts of the Hand from one Extremity of the Finger-board to the other, accompanied with Contortions of the Head and Body, and all other fuch Tricks rather belong to the Profeffors of Legerdemain and Pofture-mafters than to the Art of Mufick, the Lovers of that Art are not to expect to find any thing of that Sort in this Book. But I flatter myfelf they will find in it whatever is Neceffary for the Inftitution of a juft and regular Performer on the Violin. This Book will alfo be of Ufe to Performers on the Violoncello, and in fome Sort to thofe who begin to ftudy the Art of Compofition.

After the feveral Examples, I have added twelve Pieces in different Stiles for a Violin and Violoncello with a thorough Bafs for the Harpfichord. I have not given any Directions for the performing them ; becaufe I think the Learner will not need any, the foregoing Rules and Examples being fufficient to qualify him to perform any Mufick whatfoever.

I have nothing farther to add, but to beg the Favour of all Lovers of Mufick to receive this Book with the fame Candour that it is offered to them, by their

Moft obedient humble Servant,

F. G.

Example I.

(A.)

A Reprefents the Finger-board of a Violin, on which are marked all the Tones and Semitones, within the Compafs of that Inftrument, according to the *Diatonick* Scale; they are 23 in Number, *viz.* three Octaves and a Tone; and in every Octave of the *Diatonick* Scale there are five Tones and two of the greater Semitones. I would recommend it to the Learner, to have the Finger-board of his Violin marked in the fame Manner, which will greatly facilitate his learning to ftop in Tune.

(B.)

B fhews a Method of acquiring the true Pofition of the Hand, which is this : To place the firft Finger on the firft String upon F ; the fecond Finger on the fecond String upon C ; the third Finger on the third String upon G ; and the fourth Finger on the fourth String upon D. This muft be done without raifing any of the Fingers, till all four have been fet down ; but after that, they are to be raifed but a little Diftance from the String they touched ; and by fo doing the Pofition is perfect.

The Violin muft be refted juft below the Collar-bone, turning the right-hand Side of the Violin a little downwards, fo that there may be no Neceffity of raifing the Bow very high, when the fourth String is to be ftruck.

Obferve

Obſerve alſo, that the Head of the Violin muſt be nearly Horizontal with that Part which reſts againſt the Breaſt, that the Hand may be ſhifted with Facility and without any Danger of dropping the Inſtrument.

The Tone of the Violin principally Depends upon the right Management of the Bow. The Bow is to be held at a ſmall Diſtance from the Nut, between the Thumb and Fingers, the Hair being turned inward againſt the Back or Outſide of the Thumb, in which Poſition it is to be held free and eaſy, and not ſtiff. The Motion is to proceed from the Joints of the Wriſt and Elbow in playing quick Notes, and very little or not at all from the Joint of the Shoulder ; but in playing long Notes, where the Bow is drawn from one End of it to the other, the Joint of the Shoulder is alſo a little employed. The Bow muſt always be drawn parallel with the Bridge, (which can't be done if it is held ſtiff) and muſt be preſſed upon the Strings with the Fore-finger only, and not with the whole Weight of the Hand. The beſt Performers are leaſt ſparing of their Bow ; and make Uſe of the whole of it, from the Point to that Part of it under, and even beyond their Fingers. In an Upbow the Hand is bent a little downward from the Joint of the Wriſt, when the Nut of the Bow approaches the Strings, and the Wriſt is immediately ſtreightned, or the Hand rather a little bent back or upward, as ſoon as the Bow is began to be drawn down again.

One of the principal Beauties of the Violin is the ſwelling or encreaſing and ſoftening the Sound ; which is done by preſſing the Bow upon the Strings with the Fore-finger more or leſs. In playing all long Notes the Sound ſhould be begun ſoft, and gradually ſwelled till the Middle, and from thence gradually ſoftened till the End. And laſtly, particular Care muſt be taken to draw the Bow ſmooth from one End to the other without any Interruption or ſtopping in the Middle. For on this principally, and the keeping it always parallel with the Bridge, and preſſing it only with the Fore-finger upon the Strings with Diſcretion, depends the fine Tone of the Inſtrument.

(C.)

C ſhews the 7 Orders. What I mean by an Order is a certain Number of Notes which are to be played without tranſpoſing the Hand. The firſt Order contains 17 Notes, and the other ſix Orders contain no more than ſixteen.

Under the Notes of the firſt Order you will find their Names, and over the ſame Notes Figures denoting the Fingers with which they are to be ſtopped, and the Strings on which they are ſtopped.

It muſt be obſerved that between the two black Notes is the greater Semitone, and between the others is the Tone,

The Mark (o) denotes an open String.

From the firſt Order you are to begin to play.

'Tis neceſſary to place the Fingers exactly upon the Marks that belong to the Notes ; for on this depends the ſtopping perfectly in Tune,

After having been practiſed in the firſt Order, you muſt paſs on to the ſecond, and then to the third ; in which Care is to be taken that the Thumb always remain farther back than the Fore-finger ; and the more you advance in the other Orders the Thumb muſt be at a greater Diſtance till it remains almoſt hid under the Neck of the Violin.

It is a conſtant Rule to keep the Fingers as firm as poſſible, and not to raiſe them, till there is a Neceſſity of doing it, to place them ſomewhere elſe ; and the Obſervance of this Rule will very much facilitate the playing double Stops.

The fingering, indeed, requires an earneſt Application, and therefore it would be moſt prudent to undertake it without the Uſe of the Bow, which you ſhould not meddle with till you come to the 7th Example, in which will be found the neceſſary and proper Method of uſing it.

It

It cannot be fuppofed but that this Practice without the Bow is difagreable, fince it gives no Satisfaction to the Ear; but the Benefit which, in Time, will arife from it, will be a Recompence more than adequate to the Difguft it may give.

(D.)

D fhews the different Ways of ftopping the fame Note, and difcovers at the fame Time, that Tranfpofition of the Hand confifts in paffing from one Order to another.

As for Example.

If a Note ought to be ftopped by the fourth Finger on any String whatfoever, in the firft Order, and the fame Note be ftopped by the third Finger, it will pafs into the fecond Order; and if by the fecond Finger into the third; and confequently by ftopping it with the firft, it enters into the fourth Order.

On the contrary, if the firft Finger ftopping any Note whatfoever falls under the fourth Order; by ftopping the fame Note with the fecond Finger it paffes into the third; by ftopping the fame with the third, into the fecond; and finally by ftopping the fame with the fourth Finger it enters into the firft.

This is fufficient to fhew what Tranfpofition of the Hand is. I have only now to recommend a good Execution of the whole, both in rifing and falling; and great Care in conducting the Hand, as alfo in the placing the Fingers exactly on the Marks. With all thefe the Practitioner muft by Degrees acquire Quicknefs.

(E.)

E contains feveral different Scales, with the Tranfpofitions of the Hand, which ought to be made both in rifing and falling. It muft here be obferved, that in drawing back the Hand from the 5th, 4th and 3d Order to go to the firft, the Thumb cannot, for Want of Time, be replaced in its natural Pofition; but it is neceffary it fhould be replaced at the fecond Note.

A Sharp (♯) raifes the Note to which it is prefixed, a Semitone higher; as for Example, when a Sharp is prefixed to C, the Finger muft be placed in the Middle between C and D, and fo of the reft, except B and E; for when a Sharp is prefixed to either of them, the Finger muft be placed upon C and F. A Flat (♭) on the Contrary renders the Note to which it is prefixed, a Semitone lower: As for Example, when a Flat is prefixed to B the Finger muft be placed in the Middle between B and A, and fo of the Reft except F and C; for when a Flat is prefixed to either of them the Finger muft be placed upon E and B natural. This Rule concerning the Flats and Sharps is not abfolutely exact; but it is the eafieft and beft Rule that can be given to a Learner. This Mark (♮) takes away the Force of both the Sharp and the Flat and reftores the Note before which it is placed to its natural Quality.

Example II.

In This Example there are 13 Scales, compofed of the *Diatonick* and *Cromatick* Genera. Many may, perhaps, imagine that thefe Scales are meerly *Cromatic*, as they may not know that the *Cromatic* Scale muft be compofed only of the greater and leffer Semitones; and that the Octave alfo muft be devided into 12 Semitones, that is, 7 of the greater and 5 of the leffer; but the prefent 13 Scales being compofed of Tones and the greater and leffer Semitones, and the Octave containing 2 Tones, 5 of the greater Semitones and 3 of the leffer, I call them mixt.

Take

Take notice that the Sign (*ma*) ſignifies *Major* or greater, and the Sign (*mi*) *Minor* or leſſer.

The Poſition of the Fingers marked in the firſt Scale (which is that commonly practiſed) is a faulty one; for two Notes cannot be ſtopped ſucceſſively by the ſame Finger without Difficulty, eſpecially in quick Time.

Example III.

Contains 4 Scales of the *Diatonick Genus* tranſpoſed; and here, not to burthen the Memory of the Beginner, all the Flats (♭) inſtead of being marked at the beginning of the Staff, are marked immediately before the Notes which they belong to; but their true Situation may be ſeen at the End of the Staff.

Example IV.

In this Example are contained 9 Scales tranſpoſed, and compoſed of the *Diatonick* and *Cromatic Genera*; I have uſed the ſame Method of marking the Flats in the firſt eight Scales, and the Sharp in the ninth Scale, as in the former Example.

'Tis neceſſary in this Example to be very exact in obſerving the Diſtance between one Note and another, as alſo the Poſition of the Fingers, and the Tranſpoſition of the Hand. The Poſition of the Fingers in the laſt Scale is extreamly faulty and is ſet down meerly by Way of Caution to the Learner to avoid it. The Scales in this Example begin at the Mark (⌢) and are to be practiſed backward as well as forward.

Example V.

In this there are 4 *Diatonick* Scales tranſpoſed, and with different Tranſpoſitions of the Hand. Let it be obſerved that after you have practiſed them in aſcending they ſhould be practiſed alſo back again.

Example VI.

This Example contains 6 Scales compoſed both of the *Diatonick* and *Cromatic* tranſpoſed. Obſerve when the Sign (x) comes before C, your Finger muſt be put upon D; and when the ſame Sign is before F, the Finger muſt be upon G.

Example VII.

This contains 14 Scales, compoſed of all the Intervals which belong to the *Diatonick Genus*. In which are variety of Tranſpoſitions of the Hand. I muſt here remind you to let the Fingers reſt as firm as poſſible on the String, in the Manner already mentioned. Theſe Scales ſhould be executed with the Bow, and it will be therefore neceſſary to practice for ſome Days, all that is contained in the 24th Example, in order not to confound the Execution of the Fingers with that of the Bow.

Example VIII.

In this are contained 20 Scales in different Keys, very uſeful for acquiring Time and the ſtopping in Tune. Here it muſt be obſerved, that you are to execute them by drawing the Bow down and up, or up and down alternately; taking Care not to follow that wretched Rule of drawing the Bow down at the firſt Note of every Bar.

Example

Example IX.

In this Example are contained 16 Variations, moſt uſeful in Regard to Time, to the Bowing, the ſtopping in Tune and the Execution. Again you muſt be careful to keep the Fingers as firm as poſſible on the Strings, and alſo in bowing employ the Wriſt much, the Arm but little, and the Shoulder not at all.

Example X.

This Example is compoſed of Scales mixt with various Paſſages and Modulations, which are often repeated with different Tranſpoſitions of the Hand ; and is calculated to render the Labour of Practice more pleaſant.

Example XI.

This Example is tranſpoſed from the other, a Tone higher, ſo that the Melody may be ſaid to be the ſame, but the Accompanyment is quite different.

Example XII.

In order to execute this Compoſition well, 'tis neceſſary to examine very frequently the Tranſpoſitions of the Hand in it, until they are entirely impreſſed on the Mind ; and then to practice the 24th Example for acquiring the free Uſe of the Bow, and after proceed to execute this Example, which will be then found not ſo difficult as it may at firſt be thought.

Example XIII.

This Movement ought to be executed in ſuch a Manner as to reſemble an affecting Diſcourſe, and cannot be juſtly performed without having firſt well comprehended and often practiſed what is contained in the 18th Example.

Example XIV.

In this are contained 14 Scales; ſome of which are compoſed in Keys with a third *Major*, and the others in Keys with a third *Minor*. Theſe Scales ought to executed with Quickneſs, and in order to execute them well, you muſt take Care to put in Practice the Rules laid down in the 12th Example.

Example XV.

This contains the 7 Orders already mentioned, which proceed one after another without concluding or making any Cadence. Here alſo is introduced the *Cromatic* Flat, (♭) and the *Cromatic* Sharp. (♯) The Sign (⌢) ſignifies the laſt Note of the Order, and the Sign (1) the firſt Note of the ſuccceding Order, upon which the Hand is to be tranſpoſed.

I am ſenſible that the Modulation of theſe Orders is ſomewhat harſh, but however very uſeful; for a good Profeſſor of the Violin is obliged to execute with Propriety and Juſtneſs, every Compoſition that is laid before him ; but he who has never played any other Muſick than the agreeable and common Modulation, when he comes to play at Sight what is directly oppoſite to it, muſt be very much at a Loſs.

B

Example

Example XVI.

This Example shews in how many different Manners of bowing you may play 2, 3, 4, 5 and 6 Notes. As for Instance, 2 Notes may be played in 4 different Manners, 3 Notes in eight, 4 in 16, 5 in 32, and 6 in 62. It must be observed, that the Example marked with the Letter A is of 2 Notes, B, 3, C, 4, D, 5, and the Letter F, 6. The Letter (g) denotes that the Bow is to be drawn downwards ; and the Letter (s) that it must be drawn upwards. The Learner should be indefatigable in practising this Example till he has made himself a perfect Master of the Art of Bowing. For it is to be held as a certain Principle that he who does not possess, in a perfect Degree, the Art of Bowing, will never be able the render the Melody agreeable nor arrive at a Facility in the Execution.

Example XVII.

This Example only differs from the foregoing, as to what concerns Time and Composition ; in other Respects it is the same.

Example XVIII.

Contains all the Ornaments of Expression, necessary to the playing in a good Taste.

What is commonly call'd good Taste in singing and playing, has been thought for some Years past to destroy the true Melody, and the Intention of their Composers. It is supposed by many that a real good Taste cannot possibly be acquired by any Rules of Art ; it being a peculiar Gift of Nature, indulged only to those who have naturally a good Ear : And as most flatter themselves to have this Perfection, hence it happens that he who sings or plays, thinks of nothing so much as to make continually some favourite Passages or Graces, believing that by this Means he shall be thought to be a good Performer, not perceiving that playing in good Taste doth not consist of frequent Passages, but in expressing with Strength and Delicacy the Intention of the Composer. This Expression is what every one should endeavour to acquire, and it may be easily obtained by any Person, who is not too fond of his own Opinion, and doth not obstinately resist the Force of true Evidence. I would not however have it supposed that I deny the powerful Effects of a good Ear; as I have found in several Instances how great its Force is : I only assert that certain Rules of Art are necessary for a moderate Genius, and may improve and perfect a good one. To the End therefore that those who are Lovers of Musick may with more Ease and Certainty arrive at Perfection, I recommend the Study and Practice of the following Ornaments of Expression, which are fourteen in Number ; namely,

1st A plain Shake (*h*) 2d A Turn'd Shake (✦) 3d A superior Apogiatura (♪) 4th An inferior Apogiatura (♪) 5th Holding the Note (-) 6th Staccato (|) 7th Swelling the Sound (◢) 8th Diminishing the Sound (◣) 9th Piano (p.) 10th Forte (f.) 11th th. Anticipation (♪) 12th Separation (♪) 13th A Beat (//) 14th A close Shake (⌇) From the following Explanation we may comprehend the Nature of each Element in particular.

(First)   Of the PLAIN SHAKE.

The plain Shake is proper for quick Movements ; and it may be made upon any Note, observing after it to pass immediately to the ensuing Note.

(Second)   Of the TURNED SHAKE.

The turn'd Shake being made quick and long is fit to express Gaiety ; but if you make it short, and continue the Length of the Note plain and soft, it may then express some of the more tender Passions.

(Third)

(*Third*) Of the Superior APOGIATURA.

The Superior Apogiatura is fuppofed to exprefs Love, Affection, Pleafure, &c. It fhould be made pretty long, giving it more than half the Length or Time of the Note it belongs to, obferving to fwell the Sound by Degrees, and towards the End to force the Bow a little: If it be made fhort, it will lofe much of the aforefaid Qualities; but will always have a pleafing Effect, and it may be added to any Note you will.

(*Fourth*) Of the Inferior APOGIATURA.

The Inferior Apogiatura has the fame Qualities with the preceding, except that it is much more confin'd, as it can only be made when the Melody rifes the Interval of a fecond or third, obferving to make a Beat on the following Note.

(*Fifth*) Of Holding a NOTE.

It is neceffary to ufe this often; for were we to make Beats and Shakes continually without fometimes fuffering the pure Note to be heard, the Melody would be too much diverfified.

(*Sixth*) Of the STACCATO.

This expreffes Reft, taking Breath, or changing a Word; and for this Reafon Singers fhould be careful to take Breath in a Place where it may not interrupt the Senfe.

(7*th* and 8*th*) Of SWELLING and SOFTENING the SOUND.

Thefe two Elements may be ufed after each other; they produce great Beauty and Variety in the Melody, and employ'd alternately, they are proper for any Expreffion or Meafure.

(9*th* and 10*th*) Of PIANO and FORTE.

They are both extremely neceffary to exprefs the Intention of the Melody; and as all good Mufick fhould be compofed in Imitation of a Difcourfe, thefe two Ornaments are defigned to produce the fame Effects that an Orator does by raifing and falling his Voice.

(*Eleventh*) Of ANTICIPATION.

Anticipation was invented, with a View to vary the Melody, without altering its Intention: When it is made with a Beat or a Shake, and fwelling the Sound, it will have a greater Effect, efpecially if you obferve to make ufe of it when the Melody rifes or defcends the Interval of a Second.

(*Twelfth*) Of the SEPARATION.

The Separation is only defigned to give a Variety to the Melody, and takes place moft properly when the Note rifes a Second or Third; as alfo when it defcends a Second, and then it will not be amifs to add a Beat, and to fwell the Note, and then make the *Apogiatura* to the following Note. By this Tendernefs is exprefs'd.

(*Thirteenth*) Of the BEAT.

This is proper to exprefs feveral Paffions; as for Example, if it be perform'd with Strength, and continued long, it expreffes Fury, Anger, Refolution, &c. If it be play'd lefs ftrong

and

and shorter, it expresses Mirth, Satisfaction, &c. But if you play it quite soft, and swell the Note, it may then denote Horror, Fear, Grief, Lamentation, &c. By making it short and swelling the Note gently, it may express Affection and Pleasure.

(*Fourteenth*)   Of the Close SHAKE.

This cannot possibly be described by Notes as in former Examples. To perform it, you must press the Finger strongly upon the String of the Instrument, and move the Wrist in and out slowly and equally, when it is long continued swelling the Sound by Degrees, drawing the Bow nearer to the Bridge, and ending it very strong it may express Majesty, Dignity, &c. But making it shorter, lower and softer, it may denote Affliction, Fear, &c. and when it is made on short Notes, it only contributes to make their Sound more agreable and for this Reason it should be made use of as often as possible.

Men of purblind Understandings, and half Ideas may perhaps ask, is it possible to give Meaning and Expression to Wood and Wire; or to bestow upon them the Power of raising and soothing the Passions of rational Beings? But whenever I hear such a Question put, whether for the Sake of Information, or to convey Ridicule, I shall make no Difficulty to answer in the Affirmative, and without searching over-deeply into the Cause, shall think it sufficient to appeal to the Effect. Even in common Speech a Difference of Tone gives the same Word a different Meaning. And with Regard to musical Performances, Experience has shewn that the Imagination of the Hearer is in general so much at the Disposal of the Master, that by the Help of Variations, Movements, Intervals and Modulation he may almost stamp what Impression on the Mind he pleases.

These extraordinary Emotions are indeed most easily excited when accompany'd with Words; and I would besides advise, as well the Composer as the Performer, who is ambitious to inspire his Audience, to be first inspired himself; which he cannot fail to be if he chuses a Work of Genius, if he makes himself thoroughly acquainted with all its Beauties; and if while his Imagination is warm and glowing he pours the same exalted Spirit into his own Performance.

Example XIX.

In this is shewn how a single Note (in slow Time) may be executed with different Ornaments of Expressions.

Example XX.

This Example shews the Manner of Bowing proper to the Minim, Crochet-quaver and Semiquaver both in slow and quick Time. For it is not sufficient alone to give them their true Duration, but also the Expression proper to each of these Notes. By not considering this, it often happens that many good Compositions are spoiled by those who attempt to execute them.

You must observe that this Sign (⟋) denotes the Swelling of the Sound; the Sign (—) signifies that the Notes are to be play'd plain and the Bow is not to be taken off the Strings; and this (|) a Staccato, where the Bow is taken off the Strings at every Note.

Example XXI.

In this are shewn the different Way of playing Arpeggios on Chords composed of 3 or 4 Sounds. Here are composed 18 Variations on the Chords contained in N°. 1. by which the Learner will see in what the Art of executing the Arpeggio consists.

Example

Example XXII.

In this Example are contained all the double Stops between the Unifon and the Octave, and thefe again are repeated many Times with different Pofitions of the Fingers ; fo that in any Order whatfoever where any one of them is found you may know how to play it. Thofe who, with Quicknefs and Exactnefs, fhall execute this Example, will find themfelves far advanced in the Art of playing double Stops.

Example XXIII.

This contains two Compofitions of Scales of double Stops, which are thrice repeated with different Tranfpofitions of the Hand, in order to remove all Pain and Difficulty in the Practice. It muft be obferved, that after having fhifted the Hand, you muft purfue what follows in the fame Order, till the following Number points out a new Tranfpofition.

Example XXIV.

From this Example the Art of Bowing will eafily be acquired, and alfo that of playing in Time. The Letter *(g)* denotes that the Bow is to be drawn downwards ; the Letter *(s)* that it muft be drawn upwards. The Sign *(:S:)* fignifies a Repetition.

You muft (above all Things) obferve to draw the Bow down and up alternately. The Bow muft always be drawn ftrait on the Strings, and never be raifed from them in playing Semi-quavers. This Practice of the Bow fhould be continued, without attempting any Thing elfe until the Learner is fo far Mafter of it as to be out of all Danger of forgetting it.

Before I conclude the Article of Bowing, I muft caution the Learner againft marking the Time with his Bow ; for if he once accuftoms himfelf to it, he will hardly ever leave it off. And it has a moft difagreeable Effect, and frequently deftroys the Defign of the Compofer. As for Example, when the laft Note in one Bar is joined to the firft Note of the next by a Ligature, thofe two Notes are to be played exactly in the fame Manner as if they were but one, and if you mark the beginning of the Bar with your Bow you deftroy the Beauty of the Syncopation. So in playing Divifions, if by your Manner of Bowing you lay a particular Strefs on the Note at the beginning of every Bar, fo as to render it predominant over the reft, you alter and fpoil the true Air of the Piece, and except where the Compofer intended it, and where it is always marked, there are very few Inftances in which it is not very difagreeable.

N. B. In the twentieth Example the Word *Buono,* fignifies Good ; *Mediocre,* Middling ; *Cattivo,* Bad ; *Cattivo, o Particolare,* Bad or Particular ; *Meglio,* better ; *Ottimo,* very good ; and *Peffimo,* very bad.

Eſsempio I.

Efsempio II.

Efsemp. V.

Efsempio VI

Eſsempio VII

Esſempio VIII

8

Efsempio IX

Essempio X

Efsempio XI

15

Esempio XII

Essempio XIII

Essempio XIV

Esempio XV.

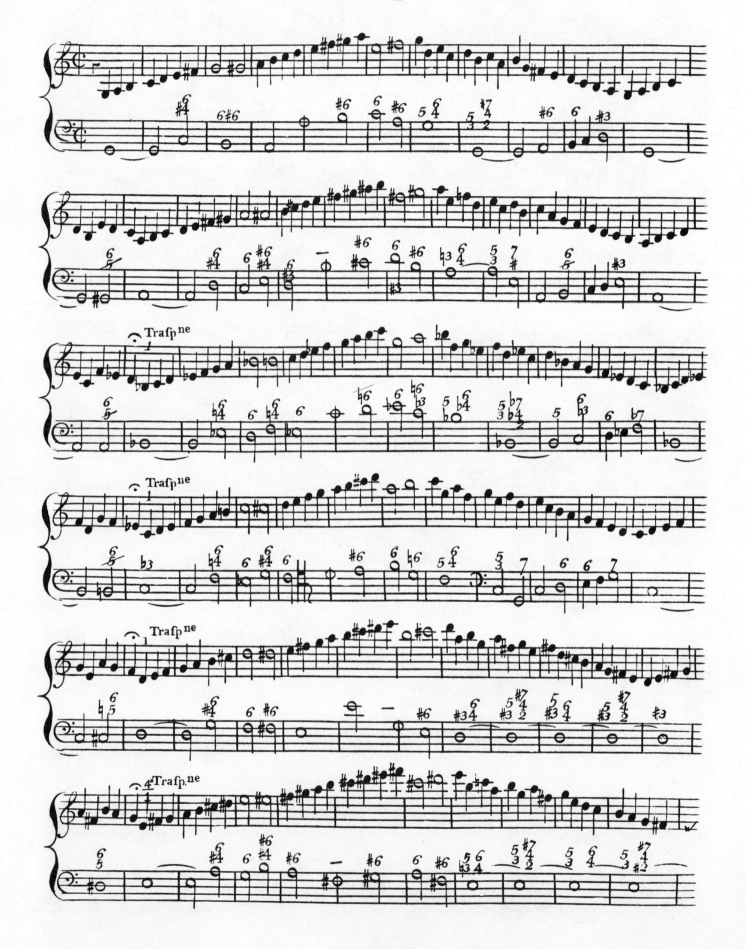

Essempio XVI

Eſsemp. XVII

Efsemp. XVIII

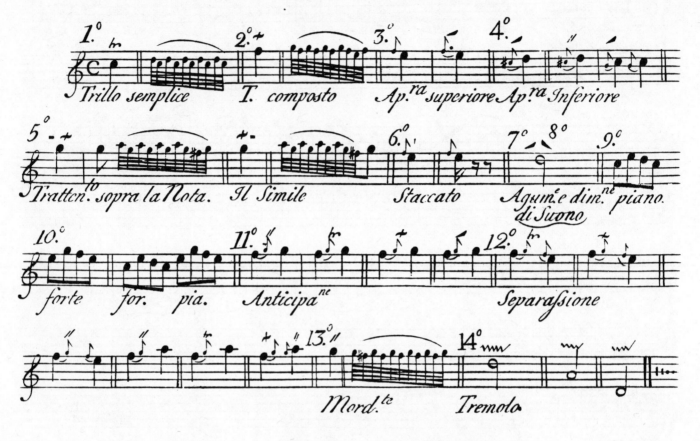

Efsemp. XIX.

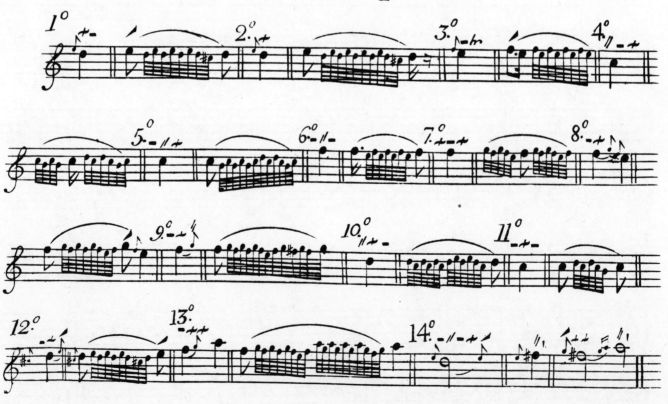

Esempio XX

Eſsemp. XXI.

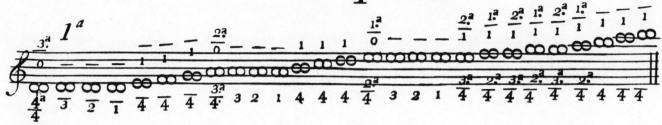

Eſsemp. XXII

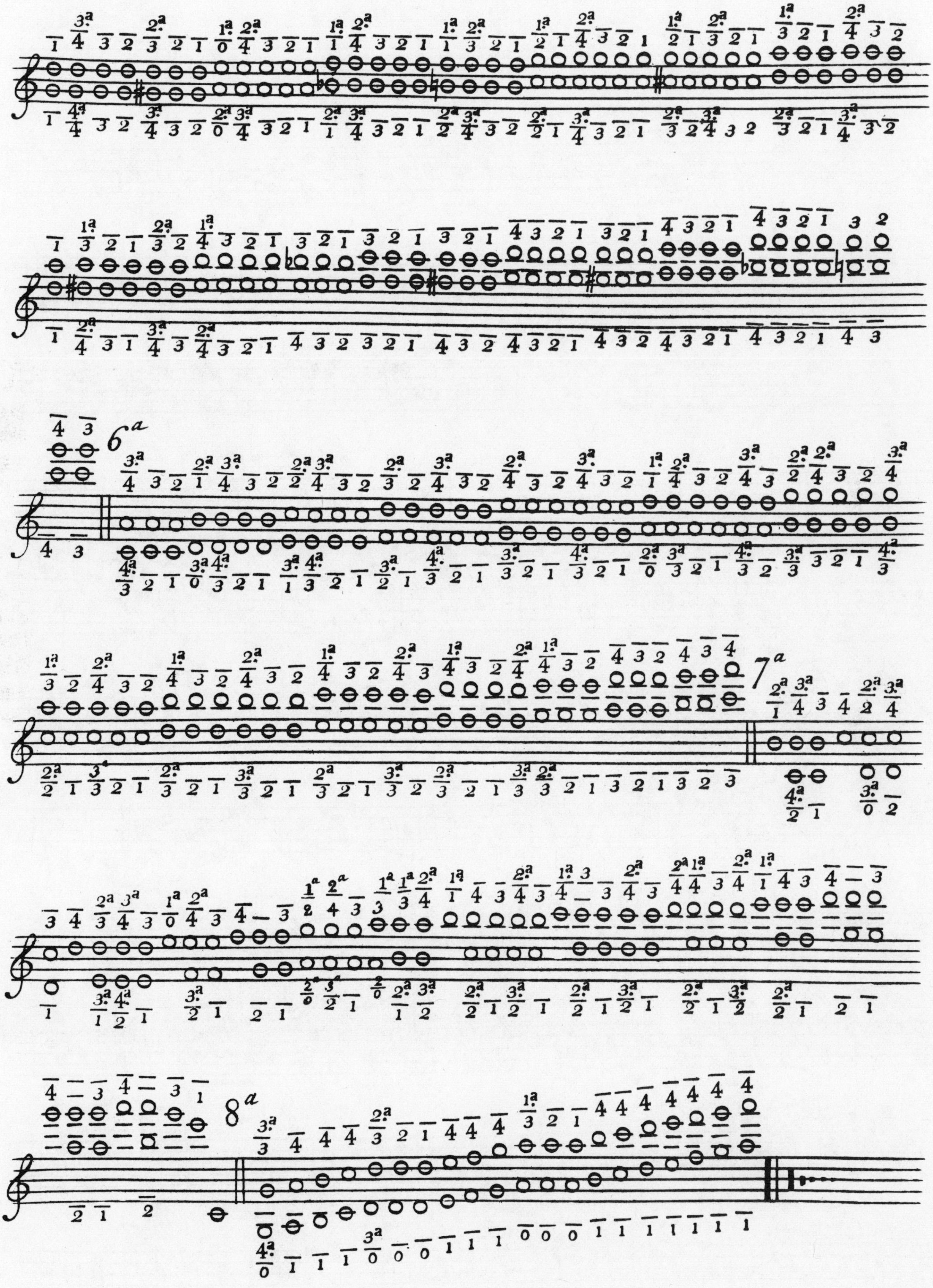
6a
7a
8a

Eſſemp. XXIII

Compoſ.ne II.

Compos.ne III.

Allegro assai

Compos.^{ne} IV.

Allo. assai

Compos.^{ne} V.

Allegro assai

Violonc.º

Compos.^ne VI.

Allegro assai

43

Compos. VIII

Compos.ne IX.

Andante moderato

non tanto   pia.   for.   pia. f.   p.

Compos.ne X

Allegro mod.to

pia.   for.   pia.   for.

Compoſ.ne XI.

Allegro aſsai

Compoſ.ⁿᵉ XII